ADHD ESSENTIALS EVERYONE NEEDS TO KNOW

Basic, Symptoms & Practical Strategies

By Aleksandra Marz B.A. (Sociology)

ADHD ESSENTIALS
EVERYONE NEEDS TO KNOW

Basics, Symptoms & Practical Strategies

By Aleksandra Marz

ISBN: 978-1-0694221-3-2

Printed in USA
First Edition 2025

This book is for informational purposes only. The author is not a medical professional, and the content should not be used as a substitute for professional medical advice, diagnosis, or treatment. Always seek the advice of a qualified healthcare provider with any questions regarding a medical condition.

The windows throughout this book aren't just as visuals. They're a quiet thread—symbols of clarity, hope, and breaking through.
For those who've felt trapped by their minds or misunderstood for years, these images are a reminder:
There's always another way to see things. Sometimes, all it takes is light coming in from the right angle.
You were never stuck. You were just waiting for the shift.

"IF I AM NOT FOR MYSELF, WHO WILL BE FOR ME?
BUT IF I AM ONLY FOR MYSELF, WHAT AM I?
AND IF NOT NOW, WHEN?"

-Rabbi Hillel

FOREWORD

Many people remain undiagnosed until adulthood because their symptoms are often internalized and misinterpreted as personality traits rather than ADHD. Over time, they learn to mask their struggles to fit in, which can lead to self-doubt, complete burnout and mental health challenges.

When I first discovered I had ADHD, in my 40s, it was like unlocking a hidden truth about myself that had been there all along. For years, I struggled with feeling like something was wrong but never had the words to explain it. It wasn't until the diagnosis that I realized I wasn't lazy, disorganized, or lacking willpower—I just had ADHD.

I finally learned that ADHD is a neurodevelopmental disorder, not a myth or the result of poor parenting, with a strong neurobiological basis that affect brain structures and its functions, influencing focus, impulse control, and emotional regulation. ADHD is highly hereditary, often running in families, and it manifests in three distinct subtypes: inattentive, hyperactive-impulsive, and combined.The statement that 'everyone has a little bit of ADHD' oversimplifies the real challenges we face, dismissing how deeply it affects our ability to function and manage stress in a demanding world.

My late diagnosis revealed a new purpose: raising ADHD awareness and helping others navigate their own journeys. Accessible diagnosis, clear guidance, resources and academic/workplace accommodations are vital, as no one should struggle alone.

I wrote this book because, truthfully, I've never been a big reader. Like many with ADHD, I find long books hard to focus on — unless I care deeply about the topic. During my own diagnosis journey, I turned to social media for short-form answers, but it often left gaps and confusion. I couldn't find a clear, compassionate resource that got straight to the point — so I created one. This guide is for people like me: people who want clarity without overwhelm. I hope it gives you the understanding I once needed, in a format that feels kind to your brain.

This journey has been about embracing my neurodivergence, realizing that being different is a source of strength that defines who I am. I hope this book help you feel seen, understood, and empowered on your unique path.

Keep it close for gentle reminders of self-awareness and self-care. Share it with your friends and family—this book can help them better understand your experiences, providing a deeper connection and the support you truly deserve. By sharing, you invite others into your world, helping create a circle of compassion and awareness.

If there's one golden rule for managing ADHD, it's this: put yourself in places that let you thrive—where your ideas spark, your energy flows, and you feel celebrated. Forcing yourself to fit where you don't belong was never the answer.

With love and understanding,

Aleksandra M

How to Use This Book Mindfully

This book isn't just for reading—it's for living...
These pages are packed with bite-sized insights designed to gently shift your awareness, build helpful habits, and spark meaningful change. Here are a few simple ways to make it part of your daily rhythm:

- *Morning Reflection*

Start your day by flipping to a random page or revisiting one that speaks to you. Reflect on its message and allow it to guide your mindset and actions. Learn one new habit weekly and stack them up!

- *Evening Journaling*

End your day with a quiet moment of reflection. Choose a page that resonates and jot down any thoughts, emotions, or patterns you noticed.
The more you understand yourself, the more you can work with your brain—not against it.

- *Share the Wisdom*

Read something that hits home? Pass it on. Share a page with a friend, partner, or family member to open up new conversations, build shared understanding and promote supportive conversations around ADHD..

EXECUTIVE DYSFUNCTION

Why can't you just start?
Because organizing, prioritizing, or planning feels like climbing Mount Everest *without gear*. Even with the best intentions, your brain hits pause, leaving you stuck at base camp.

- BODY DOUBLING

Work next to someone else, whether in person or virtually on a Zoom. Their *presence* alone will boost your focus and motivation.

- CHUNK IT DOWN

Break your projects into manageable, bite-sized pieces. for example, instead of writing an entire report in one go, start by outlining the main points or drafting just the introduction. Focusing on one small piece at a time can make the entire task feel less intimidating, and help you gain momentum.

- TIME BLOCKING

Divide your day into focused time slots for specific tasks or activities:

9:00–9:30 AM: Answer emails
9:30–10:30 AM: Work on project
10:30–10:45 AM: Take a break

It's like giving your brain a roadmap, cutting out decision fatigue and keeping you on track.

PROCRASTINATION

It's not laziness! It's the struggle of really wanting to start but feeling stuck in an invisible glue of overwhelm, distractions, and endless *"I'll do it after this one thing..."* You actually burn out from just *thinking* about all the little things you need to do.

- DOPAMINE MENU

Feel stuck? Do something completely random. Blast your favorite hype song (think *Eye of the Tiger*), shout out a silly word (BANNANAMAMA!), do 5 jumping jacks, or splash your face with cold water—anything to break that Freeze loop!

- START SMALL

Forget the whole task—commit to just 5 minutes. Once you're rolling, momentum has your back. Break things down into "must do", "should do", and "would be nice" categories—it's ADHD-friendly prioritizing.

- TAG A FRIEND

Text a friend with this challenge: "*I'm starting* [specific task] *now and will finish it in* [exact time]. *Hold me to it!*" Accountability works like magic—I invite you to try it!

HYPERFOCUS

Getting *SO* deeply absorbed in something you love that you *crush it*—sometimes squeezing a week's worth of work into just 4 hours—and the time *disappears*!

- SET ALARMS

Ever found yourself spending eight straight hours designing a logo and forgetting lunch entirely? Set alarms to snap out of the hyperfocus zone when needed.

- SET YOURSELF UP FOR SUCCESS

Keep snacks, water, and a sticky note that says "*Take a break, genius*" nearby. Make self-care unavoidable so you can refuel, stay sharp, and keep the momentum alive.

- CHANNEL IT FOR DEEP WORK

Use hyperfocus to tackle creative or challenging tasks that need intense attention. Mastering hyperfocus doesn't mean turning it off—it's about steering it where you want to go. Make it work for you!

FORGETFULNESS

It isn't just about forgetting to respond to your text/call —it's misplacing important tasks, losing track of time, or blanking on *why* we walked into a room, all while vividly remembering random, useless details.

It's not that we don't care; it's that our brains are **working overtime** just to keep up with everything neurotypical brains seem to handle on autopilot.

- LAUNCHPAD MAGIC

Set up a "**drop zone**" by the door for essentials like keys, wallet, or headphones. Ever searched your whole house for keys only to find them in the fridge? This simple trick saves you from those panic moments, and it's easier to grab & go, a game changer!

- DIGITAL "VIP" REMINDERS

Set alerts with engaging, attention-grabbing titles like "*Hey, Boss! Don't miss your 2 PM meeting.*" Fun reminders are harder to ignore and make important tasks feel exciting instead of stressful.

- VISUAL CUES

Place reminders where you'll see them. Use sticky notes on your fridge, a marker on your mirror, or even a lock screen reminder on your phone. Change them up periodically to keep them effective, as over time, familiar cues can fade into the background.

TASK SWITCHING STRUGGLE

Feeling **stuck** while trying to shift focus from one task to another— especially when you're ***super into*** what you're doing (even if it's not helpful anymore).

- TRANSITION WITH INTENTION

Take five deep breaths or stretch before switching tasks. These mindful pauses signal your brain it's time to shift gears.

- MINDFUL MOVEMENT

Reset with a few goofy yoga poses or move how your body wants—random bursts of energy can flip the switch from dread to motivation. Bonus points if you throw on a hype song! Think: "*Who Run the World? Girls*!" This boosts energy and prepares your brain for the next task.

- GET A VISUAL TIMER

Set visual timers to block out specific task times. This creates a sense of urgency and structure, aiding in smoother transitions.

SQUIRREL MODE

When your attention gets pulled by anything *shiny* or *new*, leading to constant **distraction**. It's truly unintentional and can derail your focus entirely, leaving your original task *forgotten* like yesterday's leftovers—and your conversations taking *wild detours* mid-sentence.

- DISTRACTION DUMP

When you're mid-task and your brain shouts "*Ooh, shiny*!"—write down those distractions in a "later" notebook or app to return to them.
It frees your mind to stay on task without fearing you'll forget that brilliant, unrelated idea!

- SOUND BUBBLE

Pop on noise-canceling headphones or set up a workspace that feels like your focus zone or create a designated workspace to stay grounded. This signals your brain that it's time to tune in and get things done, not drift away.

- VISUAL ZEN

Declutter your workspace/home to minimize visual noise. A clean desk or room can help keep your mind clear and focused.
Less external chaos = more internal calm and mental clarity.

BRAIN FOG

That hazy, sluggish feeling where your thoughts feel like they're moving through mud—it's your brain's way of saying: *"I need to rest..."*

- COLD EXPOSURE

Shock your brain awake with a splash of cold water on your face or a quick cold shower. Feeling bold? Dunk your face in ice water for 10 seconds and watch the fog clear.
It activates your vagus nerve and gives your system a clean mental reset—like hitting refresh on your browser.

- BODY SHAKING OR DANCING

Shake off the fog—literally! Stand up and shake your body or break into a 1-minute wild dance party. It's weird, but it works!
Moving your body increases circulation and helps reboot your mental energy fast.

- CAFFEINE NAP

Drink a cup of coffee and immediately set a 20-minute nap timer. By the time you wake up, the caffeine kicks in, and you're ready to roll.

BRAIN FREEZE

Suddenly going blank or freezing up when overwhelmed or under pressure, as if your brain needs a moment to reboot, but usually at the worst time.

- BOX BREATHING

Inhale, hold, exhale, and pause for 4 seconds at each step. Repeat a few times! Perfect for those moments when your brain feels like it's buffering —it's quick, simple, and calms your mind instantly.

- PROGRESSIVE MUSCLE RELAXATION

Tense each muscle group for 5 seconds, then release. Start from your toes and move upward—this melts tension fast.
It helps reconnect you to your body and signals your brain that you're safe to relax and refocus.

- GROUNDING EXERCISE

Name 5 things you can see, hear, or feel around you. This **anchors** you in the present and helps unfreeze your thoughts. Or, if you're in a conversation, own the moment with some humor: *"Oops, I had the perfect thing to say, but it ran away. Bear with me until my brain reboots."*

OBJECT PERMANENCE

"*Out of sight, out of mind*"—is the ADHD mantra. If it's not right in front of us, it practically doesn't exist. This can mean forgotten tasks, misplaced items, unintentionally ghosting people, or a bag of produce *quietly* spoiling in the back of the fridge.

- CLEAR BINS AND LABELS

Use transparent containers and labels to keep items visible but organized.This keeps essentials in plain view so they don't disappear from your mental radar.

- VISUAL CUES

Keep reminders in high-traffic areas like the fridge, doors, bathroom mirrors, or phone screens to ensure you don’t forget important tasks, items, or people. (How about a sticky note on your coffee maker that says, "*Grab your lunch for work!*")

- SET RELATIONSHIP REMINDERS

Schedule weekly reminders on your calendar to check in with loved ones—text a friend, call your family. It keeps connections alive even when they're not in your immediate view.
It may feel robotic at first but it builds real emotional consistency overtime.

ALL-OR-NOTHING THINKING

Why do anything *halfway* when you can go all in *or* avoid it entirely?
The ADHD brain loves extremes—it's simple, but finding balance? That's the real challenge.

- PRACTICE PROGRESS OVER PERFECTION

Remember, "*80% done is better than 100% perfect.*" Small wins build momentum, and finishing something—even imperfectly—feels amazing. Each step forward still gets you closer than standing still.

- EMBRACE THE GREY

Life isn't black and white—there's a whole spectrum between perfection and failure. Celebrate the middle ground, because it's those small actions that make a big difference over time.

Hit "*send*" on a text even if it's not perfectly worded, or wear a bold lipstick even if the rest of your look isn't flawless.

- FLEXIBLE GOAL SETTING

Set goals that can bend without breaking. Life happens, and plans change—give yourself permission to **adapt**. It's better to shift gears than to abandon the whole thing because it didn't go perfectly!

COGNITIVE DRIFT

It's when your mind wanders and your thoughts take surprise detours into daydreams or random ideas, often during conversations—it's *creativity* at work—just not always at the right time.

- REPHRASE AND REFLECT

"Wait, let me make sure I got this right..." Simple, but game-changing. Summarize or repeat back what the other person just said. Not only does it show active listening, but it also keeps your ADHD brain grounded in the conversation.

- DYNAMIC WORKSPACE

Alternate between sitting and standing desks or move your work to a cozy café to shake up your energy and focus. A simple shift of space can turn a zoning-out moment into a productive work session.

- THOUGHT PARKING

During conversations or tasks, write down wandering ideas or unrelated thoughts in a notebook. This will help clear your mental space and allow you to re-engage fully.
It reassures your brain that the thought is safe and can be returned to later—no need to chase it now.

PERFECTIONISM

Getting stuck in an endless loop of overthinking, trying to nail every tiny detail "*just right*," until starting feels way more terrifying than messing up. Instead of risking mistakes, you freeze up and procrastinate, **paralyzed** by the fear of falling short of perfection. *Classic ADHD spiral!*

- EMBRACE IMPERFECTION

Intentionally make small, harmless mistakes in low-stakes tasks, like sending an email without triple-checking every word. It trains your brain to let go of the fear of being less than perfect.

- SHARE EARLY, GET REAL

Show your work in progress to a friend—they'll point out what's awesome, not the tiny "flaws" you're obsessing over.
Getting it out of your head and into the world breaks the perfectionism loop and builds creative confidence.

- SET 'GOOD ENOUGH' GOALS

Redefine success by asking, "*What's the minimum this task needs to get done well?*" Stop chasing perfection and start finishing things faster.
Remind yourself: "*Done is better than perfect, and I'm allowed to celebrate progress, not just perfection.*"

"MIGHT NEED LATER" MENTALITY

Refusing to close computer tabs, delete apps, or discard notes because something *important* could be there that you *might* need someday...

It's a mix of optimism ("*I'll get back to this soon*") and anxiety ("*What if I can't find it again?*"). Deleting screenshots feels like losing an opportunity, even if it's one you're unlikely to revisit.

- "MIGHT NEED LATER" FOLDER

Create a special folder and save tabs or apps here. Set expiration dates—if you don't revisit, **delete** guilt-free. Future-you won't even remember it was there.
(This gives your brain permission to let go without the fear of losing something important.)

- EMBRACE DIGITAL DECLUTTERING

Skip the chaos and keep a lighthearted attitude! Use one master app for all notes with tags like "*Pending*", "*Archive*", or "*Maybe Later*". Got 37 tabs open "*just in case*"? Close half of them, delete unused apps, or tidy up random files.

- AFFIRM

"I trust that the right ideas and tools will find their way back to me when needed. I'm ***letting go*** *to create space for clarity and inspiration."*

INTERNAL COMMENTARY

That constant inner voice of ideas, to-do lists, random thoughts, and worries all *buzzing* in your head, leaving you feeling mentally exhausted even when you haven't physically done much. It can pull your attention in a *million* directions, making it so tough to stay focused.

- NAME YOUR INNER CRITIC

Give that nagging voice a persona ("*Hi, Negative Nancy!* No offense to the awesome Nancys out there"). It creates distance between you and your thoughts, making them feel less overwhelming or personal.
(Bonus: say your response out loud—hearing your confident rebuttal overrides the negative cycle in your brain!)

- WRITE IT OUT/JOURNALING

Got the same thought looping in your head? Clear the mental clutter by writing down everything swirling in your head. No filter, no structure—just dump it out and breathe easier.

- PAUSE THE MENTAL NOISE

When your inner critic gets loud, take a mini "*mental vacation*" by changing your environment. Step outside for a quick walk, grab a refreshing drink, or even do something physical to break the mental loop. Shifting gears can help reset your brain and create space for calmer thoughts.

OVERTHINKING

When your brain refuses to hit the "**off**" switch, overthinking takes the wheel, spiraling into endless loops of second-guessing what-ifs, could-haves, and should-haves.

It's like your mind is **stuck** *buffering* on a thought.

- EMBRACE IMPERFECTION

Ever baked cookies that came out a little wonky but still tasted amazing? That's the energy! Intentionally complete a task without obsessing over every detail to remind yourself that done is better than perfect. Imperfections add *charm.* PRACTICE!

- TIME-LIMIT YOUR WORRIES

Set a 10-minute timer to overthink or spiral wildly. When the timer goes off, shift focus and move on! Bonus: Scheduling dedicated worry time can help you avoid dwelling throughout the day. Overthinking is just a time thief, and your brain's got way better things to do!

- DELIGHTFUL DISTRACTIONS

When your brain is spiraling into overthinking, give yourself full permission to hit the mental reset button. Watch a hilarious video, dive into a random game, or do something completely absurd and unrelated. This isn't avoiding the issue—it's recharging our mind.

ANALYSIS PARALYSIS

The moment *overthinking* meets the fear of making the *wrong choice*, and it turns every decision into a mental marathon—leaving you either stuck like a frozen browser or so drained that you grab the iffy option just to escape the **overwhelm**.

Often tied to perfectionism, it's the struggle to act without being 100% sure you'll get it right.

- SET A TIMER

Give yourself 5 minutes to decide. Still stuck? Flip a coin and let fate decide...Yes, **seriously**! The best part? You'll realize what you really wanted mid-air.
A deadline shrinks the decision space and helps your brain shift from spinning to choosing.

- BODY DOUBLE DECISION-MAKING

Call a friend, coworker, or even your dog (no judgment). Talking it out—or just having someone around—helps break the loop.

- MAKE THE WORST CHOICE FIRST

Sounds risky, right? But hear me out: Pick what you think is the worst option and roll with it. It sounds wild, but it gets you moving—and action leads to clarity. Once you're in motion, you'll either surprise yourself or quickly spot the better path.

RUMINATION

Getting stuck in a mental loop, replaying the *same* thoughts over and over without solving anything—it's like your brain's on repeat with no "***off***" button.

- MANTRA MAGIC

Break the cycle with a bold empowering statement like, "*I run this mind and not the other way around.*" Say it like you mean it—**on repeat**—until those thoughts know who's boss.

- SENSORY BOOST

Snap yourself out of overthinking with a quick sensory reset—suck on a sour candy, hold an ice cube to your neck, or blast your favorite upbeat song.
A sharp sensation can break the loop and pull you back into the present moment.

- TRY SOMETHING NEW

Shift your brain out of autopilot with a fresh activity. Whip up a crazy recipe you've never dared to try, put on a playlist that's way out of your usual vibe, or take a random left turn on your daily walk.

RAPID COGNITION

Your brain connects dots *faster* than Wi-Fi—bursting with ideas, patterns, and solutions no one else sees. It's an amazing *superpower*… until the speed leaves you craving an "off" switch.

- CAPTURE THE SPARK

Inspiration strikes fast—be ready. Use voice-to-text apps or jot quick notes on your phone. No filters, no judgment—just pure, unfiltered brilliance!

- MAKE IT YOUR SUPERPOWER

Ride the wave—use that burst of energy strategically! Rapid cognition is your secret weapon for a quick win. Channel it into brainstorming or problem-solving, and watch those racing thoughts turn into phenomenal solutions.

- CREATE "IDEA PARKING LOTS"

When your mind is bouncing between ideas faster than you can manage, write them down in a designated space—your "parking lot." This allows you to acknowledge every thought without losing focus on your current task. Later, revisit the parking lot and see which ideas are worth pursuing further.

REJECTION SENSITIVITY DYSPHORIA— RSD

Feeling deeply hurt by small signs of even perceived criticism or rejection, as if your emotional volume is **set to max.**

It's one of the most painful and misunderstood aspects of ADHD, leaving you second-guessing yourself, avoiding risks, and often trapped in a spiral of self-doubt...

- NAME THE FEELING

When RSD hits, stop and name it: "*This is rejection sensitivity, not reality.*" It helps you separate emotion from fact. Picture yourself as a detective, searching for actual evidence of rejection—spoiler: it's usually not there.

- BUILD A SUPPORTIVE NETWORK

Surround yourself with people that understand your sensitivities. Share your RSD experience with trusted friends or a partner who can validate your feelings and remind you of the truth when emotions cloud your perspective.

- EXPERIMENT WITH REJECTION

Challenge yourself with bold, unexpected requests to build resilience. For instance, ask a stranger for a small favor, like borrowing their pen , or request a free sample at a store. This unconventional approach can **reframe** rejection as a growth opportunity.

EMOTIONAL ROLLERCOASTER

With ADHD, emotions can flip *faster* than channels on a remote—one moment you're fine, the next you're overwhelmed, all because of a *small trigger* that can feel huge as if it's the final drop in an already full bucket.

- PAUSE FOR GRATITUDE

When emotions spiral—use this tiny reset that feels surprisingly **grounding**: pause and think of 3 things you're thankful for—like that cozy hoodie you're wearing, the sun shining outside, or your favorite snack waiting for you.

- REACH OUT FOR CONNECTION

Feeling shaky? Call a friend who gets you or grab a hug from someone nearby. Sometimes, a simple "*ugh, today's wild*" conversation, or a quick squeeze can melt the tension away.

- TRY "EMOTIONAL OFFLOAD"

Record yourself ranting (*privately*!) about what's on your mind. Watching it back can feel surprisingly **validating** and help you process emotions more effectively.
You are not looking for solutions—just giving your emotions somewhere to go so they don't stay stuck swirling inside you.)

EMOTIONAL HYPER-AWARENESS

Picking up on every emotional nuance—yours and others'—with such vivid intensity that it makes you *deeply* empathetic, but also leaves you *vulnerable* to emotional burnout.

- SET HEALTHY BOUNDARIES

Got a friend who vents a lot? (You know—the energy vampires...) Protect your emotional energy by saying, "*I care, but I need a little space right now.*" Remember: It's okay to step back—you don't have to fix everything.

- "ZOOM OUT" TRICK

When caught in an emotional spiral, ask yourself: "*Will this matter in a week? A month? A year?*" Shifting perspective helps cool the emotional temperature.

- SHIELDING VISUALIZATION

Picture yourself surrounded by an invisible bubble, keeping the bad vibes out but letting the good ones in. Dress yourself up in it ahead of those long, extended family gatherings. It's like having your own personal filter to stay calm and grounded in challenging environments.

NEGATIVE SELF-TALK

That inner voice? Loud, relentless, *rarely kind*, and obsessed with pointing out how neurotypical people seem to have it all together. It drags you into guilt and shame, pretending it's helpful—but really, it's just comparing *apples to oranges*.

- FLIP THE SCRIPT

When a negative thought hits, learn to put it down, flip it, and reverse it. Now, cross it out like a bad lyric and remix it into something empowering. Example: "*I always mess up*" turns into "*I'm doing my best, and that's enough.*" Bonus: make it playful; **post** your new mantra somewhere you'll see daily!

- FIND YOUR CREW

Surround yourself with people who lift you up—whether it's real-life friends or online communities that just get you. Join a group chat, follow uplifting creators, or find a safe space to share your wins and struggles. Remember, good vibes are contagious!

- VALIDATE THE WINS

Keep a "Hype File" (a notebook or digital folder) where you save compliments, accomplishments, or kind messages. When self-doubt creeps in, flip through it and remind yourself of how far you've come.

SOCIAL BURNOUT

That "*peopled out*" feeling when you've hit your interaction limit, and alone time becomes non-negotiable and the only way to recharge (Although sometimes, you'll turn on a TV—not to watch, but to feel less lonely).

- MICRODOSE SOCIALIZING

Not every hangout needs to be a three-hour event. Create low-pressure ways to stay connected, like a quick coffee catch-up or joining a friend for a short walk.

- RECHARGE BEFORE & AFTER

Prep for social events with self-care rituals—take a quiet moment, practice deep breathing, or listen to your favorite calming music beforehand. After a group dinner, schedule recharge time and decompress with your favorite show to reset.

- PRACTICE "NO" WITHOUT OVEREXPLAINING

Sometimes a simple "*Can't make it, sorry!*" is all you need. Whenever you prefer to attend but want flexibility, communicate your needs upfront: "*Hey, I'd love to come, but I might leave early when I'm feeling low on energy.*"
Setting expectations this way avoids awkward exits and keeps things comfortable for everyone.

EMPATHIC INTUITION

As highly sensitive people, our ADHD brains act like *emotional radars*, strangely picking up on what others are thinking, feeling, and needing with remarkable accuracy. It's a powerful *gift*, but without boundaries, it can easily lead to emotional overwhelm or burnout.

- READ THE ROOM LIKE A PRO

You know that gut feeling when something's off? Trust it. Use your knack for sensing emotions to navigate tricky conversations or support someone who's struggling without them having to say a word.

- PAUSE BEFORE YOU JUMP IN

Empathy isn't about fixing someone's problems—it's about showing they're not alone in how they feel. Next time someone vents, do this: pause, listen, and respond with "*That sounds tough.*" It validates more than advice ever could.

- CHANNEL EMPATHY THROUGH VOLUNTEERING

Use this gift with **intention**—help where it's needed. Volunteer at causes that matter to you. Whether it's mentoring, community events, or lending a hand, your ability to connect deeply can make a real difference.

SOCIAL MASKING

Concealing your ADHD traits to fit in.
This isn't just exhausting—it's a constant performance that drains your energy and chips away at your sense of *self*, leaving you feeling depleted and emotionally worn out.

- AUTHENTIC EXPRESSION

Spend time with people and places where you feel safe to be yourself. Share with trusted friends or family what ADHD means for you—your struggles and strengths. Gradually practice being yourself in comfortable settings to reduce the habit of masking. Bonus: **Authenticity** attracts those who truly celebrate you.

- ENERGY MANAGEMENT

Recognize that social interactions can be draining due to the effort of masking. Allocate time for rest and recharge after social events to prevent burnout.

- SEEK SUPPORTIVE COMMUNITIES

Connect with neurodivergent communities, both online and offline, where masking is unnecessary, and authenticity is embraced. Sharing experiences can provide relief and much-needed validation. You don't have to do it alone—surrounding yourself with people who get it can make all the difference in feeling seen, supported, and understood.

SMALL TALK STRUGGLE

Surface talk is widely disliked by ADHDers—it can feel boring, scary, unnecessary, or just plain difficult. We often disconnect or start planning our escape, craving *depth* and *meaningful* conversations instead.

- PREPARE A FEW GO-TO QUESTIONS

-"*Random question, but have you seen anything lately that totally blew your mind?*"
-"*Okay, real question—what's one thing that made you smile today?*"
-"*Have you tried that new (restaurant/show) yet?*"

- OWN YOUR REALNESS

Small talk can feel like torture for ADHD brains craving deeper convos. Skip the fluff—steer the chat toward stuff that actually excites you. Instead of "*So, what do you do?*" try, "*What's something you're really into right now?*"

- SHIFT THE SPOTLIGHT

Turn the conversation to them with genuine curiosity—they'll love the attention, and you'll feel less pressure. Try asking, "*What's something exciting you've been working on lately?*" or "*What's your favorite way to unwind after a long day? That's interesting! Tell me more about it...*"

SOCIAL ANXIETY

Misreading social cues, leading to awkward moments or misunderstandings that can make socializing feel like a *minefield*.

If you're already planning how to act tomorrow, just know you're not the only one—and you've totally got this!

- BRING YOUR SOCIAL SIDEKICK

Have a friend who gets your vibe tag along to help you feel less out of place.Whether they jumpstart conversations or just hang out, their presence will ease the pressure.

- PREPARE A "SOCIAL SCRIPT"

Before heading out, brainstorm 2-3 go-to topics or questions to kick off conversations, like asking someone about their favorite travel spot, what podcast they're into, or if they've tried any good food spots lately. Think of it as your "*social cheat sheet.*"

- GRADUAL EXPOSURE

Create a "fear ladder" of social situations, from easiest to hardest. Start small—like smiling at someone or asking a simple question—and work your way up. Reflect on each experience: *Did anyone actually judge me? What went well?* Celebrate every win, no matter how small, to build confidence.

STRONG SENSE OF JUSTICE

Feeling *deeply* about fairness and driven to stand up for what's right, often fueled by empathy and a sensitivity to seeing others treated unfairly.

- REFRAME DISAGREEMENTS

When frustration hits over something that feels unfair, try this: view disagreements as chances to learn something new. Think of it like a puzzle—every piece of the other person's point of view helps you see things in a new light and grow your own perspective.

- CHANNEL YOUR PASSION

That fire you feel when something's unjust? Turn it into advocacy. Volunteer for causes you care about, sign petitions, or join grassroots movements. You'll not only make a difference but also feel the deep satisfaction of standing up for what truly matters to you.

- PICK YOUR BATTLES

Accept that not all battles can be won—focus on what you *can* change. Ask, "*Is this worth my energy?*" Imagine the relief of focusing on causes where you can make the biggest difference without feeling burnt out.

IMPOSTER SYNDROME

Doubting *your own* success or abilities, even when you're clearly nailing it, as if at any moment someone might pull back the curtain and expose you.

• BE AWARE OF YOUR INNER CRITIC

Pay attention when limiting self-talk creeps in—phrases like, "*I'm not good enough,*" or, "*I'll be exposed.*" Replace them with bold truths: "*I am skilled, resilient, and* ***absolutely*** *earned my place here.*" Over time, this rewiring helps build an inner voice that supports you instead of sabotaging you.

• CALL YOUR HYPE PERSON

Reach out to someone who sees your brilliance. A quick reminder of your greatness from them can be the exact spark you need to shut down the doubt and step back into your power. Let their words anchor you in reality when your brain tries to tell you otherwise.

• CRUSH IT WITH SMALL WINS

Big goals feeling overwhelming? Break them down into manageable tasks. Every step you complete proves you're on track and unstoppable—momentum is yours for the taking.

TACTLESS HONESTY

Blurting out what's on your mind feels right—because why wouldn't people want the truth? But sometimes your unfiltered thoughts can **sting**, even when your heart's in the right place.

- PRACTICE THE 3-SECOND PAUSE

Before unleashing your brilliance, take a breath. In those glorious three seconds, you can choose whether to drop truth bombs or throw out a softer, kinder version. Instead of saying, "*That outfit does nothing for you*"—try: "*That color would make you look like a million bucks!*" Still honest but kinder.

- USE "I" STATEMENTS

Frame feedback from your perspective to avoid defensiveness. Instead of "*You never listen,*" try, "*I feel unheard.*" "*I'm overwhelmed with too much at once*" works better than "Why do you keep dumping tasks on me?" Keeps it real, **minus** the conflict.

- SEEK CONSENT BEFORE GIVING FEEDBACK

Ask if they're up for the raw truth or if they'd rather you soften it up. It shows you care about how it lands, not just what you say.

OVERSHARING

Revealing too much personal information in the moment because impulsivity and emotional excitement team up and forget to hit the brakes. Whether it's a casual chat **or** a first date, we just have a strong need to feel *deeply* understood. We will overshare at a social gathering and then spend weeks thinking that we were too much and now everyone dislikes us.

- PAUSE + SIP TECHNIQUE

Always keep a drink in your hand (coffee, water—whatever works). Before diving into your personal saga, take a sip. It gives you a moment to think, "Do I really need to overshare right now?" Bonus: You'll stay hydrated and look extra classy while doing it!

- SEEK FEEDBACK

Ask your friends or family for their "*no filter*" feedback on your communication habits. They'll let you know if you're oversharing or if you should start your own podcast!

- PRACTICE ACTIVE LISTENING

Really hear what the other person is saying—no, seriously, actually listen. It's a game-changer for the convo and helps you resist the urge to turn it into a one-person show of your life story. Only dive deeper if they're vibing with you and opening up too!

STORY MATCHING

Hearing someone share a personal traumatic story and feeling the urge to respond with your own **similar** experience. It isn't about seeking attention—it's a way of *finding validation* through shared struggles and making a heartfelt effort to *connect* and foster understanding.

- LISTEN LIKE A PRO

Focus on their story without plotting your own response. Practice active listening to show empathy without taking over. Try: "*How did you feel when that happened?*" or "*What did you do next?*"

- VALIDATION 101

You don't always need to share your own story to connect—sometimes a **simple** "*Wow, I hear you*" says it all!

- BE OPEN ABOUT STORY MATCHING

Let your loved ones know that story matching is your way of processing ADHD and showing you care. It's a natural response, and being open about it helps them understand you better and offer the support you need.

SPONTANEOUS OVERCOMMITMENT

Saying "*yes!*" to too many things with *enthusiasm* in the moment, only to feel **overwhelmed** later when your time and energy can't keep up.

- **HIT PAUSE BEFORE COMMITTING**

When something new pops up, take a breath. Ask yourself: *"Can I handle this right now, or am I already juggling five other things?"* A quick pause can save you from the chaos of biting off more than you can chew.

- **CELEBRATE SAYING NO**

Saying "***NO***" is an act of self-respect, creating space for what truly aligns with your values and priorities. It's not just about what you avoid, but what you make room for.

- **"IS THIS WORTH MY TIME?" CHECKLIST**

Before saying yes to anything, ask yourself: *Does this match my goals? Do I have the time? Will it leave me wondering why I said yes while scrolling through Netflix later?* If it doesn't pass the vibe check, politely decline.

TIME BLINDNESS

Time feels like a slippery concept—either it's dragging endlessly or vanishing in a blink, making it almost *impossible* to manage without alarms, timers, or last-minute panic.

- TIMERS: YOUR PERSONAL ASSISTANT

Set alarms for tasks, breaks, and even snacks—because let's face it, if your phone isn't yelling at you, it's not happening. And let's get honest—do you really think you'll arrive on time without adding buffer space?

- VISUAL SCHEDULES—YOUR LIFELINE

If it's not in your face, it doesn't exist. Color-coded calendars, sticky notes, or giant whiteboards make your plans impossible to ignore. Bonus: Add buffer time to every appointment or project—and reward yourself—with a healthy smoothie if you actually make it on time!

- TRY TIME-BLOCKING

Assign chunks of time for specific tasks to give your day structure. ADHD brains love clear instructions—this helps you stay focused, keeps you from drifting off, and makes the busiest day much more manageable (*hello to built-in breaks!*).

THE DOOM PILE

That intimidating heap of unsorted stuff (papers, laundry, etc.) that grows into a mountain as you avoid it for a **temporary** stress relief.
Clearing the pile can feel like clearing your mind, offering a sense of control.

- FOCUS ON IMMEDIATE WINS

Tackle "*hot spots*" like your desk, bedside table, or kitchen counter—places that impact your daily life the most.

- CREATE ZONES OF POWER

Set up spots for specific tasks—like a "*work zone*," "*chill zone*," or "*miscellaneous*." Your ADHD brain will associate each space with **one** purpose, cutting chaos, reducing decision fatigue, and keeping things functional. Mental cheat code for productivity!

- THE ULTIMATE CLUTTER ATTACK PLAN

— Use **clear** bins and bold labels to stop the mystery box madness.
—"*Do I Really Need This?*" If you haven't used it in a **year**, it's officially time to let it go. (Sentimental Items: Keep one meaningful piece and take a photo of the rest.)
—Start with **one** area and challenge yourself to ditch 5-10 things in 10 minutes. You'll feel like a hero while making quick progress.
— Grab a **friend**, and let them keep you on track. You'll both laugh, argue over what to toss, and get stuff done.
— Declutter as You Go and Make it a **daily** habit (tackle the mess before it tackles you)!

NEVER-ENDING TO-DO LIST

You've got **big** dreams, **big** plans, and a to-do list that *never* shrinks. It's not laziness; it's just hard to prioritize what actually matters when everything feels urgent.

- PRIORITIZE YOUR LIST

Stop staring at a giant list and pick the top 3 things that matter most today. Rank your tasks by urgency or importance.Clarity cuts through overwhelm—when everything isn't urgent, your brain can finally breathe.

- USE THE 2-MINUTE RULE

If it'll take less than 2 minutes, **do it now**! The tiny tasks pile up fast, and before you know it, that 2-minute thing has turned into an hour of frustration. Take care of it, and move on.

- DELEGATE

Not every task is yours to bear. Pass on what you can—delegate, outsource, or ask for help. Freeing up your time increases your efficiency and keeps you from carrying unnecessary weight.

TIME OPTIMISM

Thinking you've got **plenty** of time to finish something, only to realize *too late* that you *don't*—ADHD's hopeful but often unreliable timekeeper.

- START BY RECOGNIZING IT

Acknowledge that your internal clock often underestimates time—adjust accordingly. Admit it—you're convinced you can finish a month's worth of work in an hour. Your internal clock is like that friend who's always late but swears they're "*just around the corner*".

- VISUAL TIME MANAGEMENT TOOLS

Buy a Pomodoro clock—it's like watching time slowly disappear, but in a chill, non-terrifying way. Set it up, zone in, and stop stressing—just let the minutes slip away while you crush your task!

- BUFFER ZONES

Add a 50% cushion to every task. Think your task will take 30 minutes? Give yourself an extra 15, in case life throws a plot twist. It's like packing snacks for a trip—you'll thank yourself when things run over!

LAST-MINUTE PRODUCTIVITY

That *magical* burst of focus and energy when a deadline approaches, proving you can be incredibly productive... under **maximum** pressure.

- HARNESS YOUR ADRENALINE

Set earlier "*fake deadlines*" to trick your brain into thinking it's crunch time. When the clock's ticking, the panic sets in. Use that adrenaline to your advantage!
(Bonus: Finishing early feels like winning a game you didn't even know you were playing.)

- BREAK TASKS INTO MICRO-DEADLINES

Big projects can feel like trying to eat a whole pizza by yourself. So, slice it up! Break it into smaller, manageable chunks instead of one massive task.

- CREATE URGENCY WITH A COUNTDOWN

Set a timer for the time you think the task will take, and race against it. The ticking clock adds pressure and helps you overcome procrastination. Even if you don't finish, you've likely done way more than if you hadn't started at all.

TASK HOPPING

Taking on a *million* tasks at *once*, fueled by ADHD-driven urgency and need for stimulation, only to have distractions turn it into a juggling act where most of the pieces end up dropping.

- VISUAL PROGRESS BOARD

Grab some sticky notes and create columns like "*To Do,*" "*In Progress,*" and "*Done.*" Moving a task to the "*Done*" column feels oddly satisfying—like your brain just hit the jackpot on the dopamine slot machine!

- LIMIT YOUR OPTIONS

Pick your top 3 tasks for the day, then hide everything else like it's a secret treasure you'll "*totally*" come back to later. Out of sight, out of mind, less overwhelm!

- ACCOUNTABILITY BUDDY

Team up with someone (virtually or in person) to tackle tasks together. Their focus rubs off on you, and you'll feel way less tempted to disappear into a TikTok rabbit hole!

P WAITING MODE

That stuck feeling where you're mentally parked and waiting on an upcoming event, leaving you unable to focus on *anything else*, as if your mind is stuck in a holding pattern.

- RECOGNIZE IT

Waiting mode isn't laziness—it's your ADHD brain stuck in a holding pattern. Acknowledge it for what it is, and you'll instantly feel less guilty. Awareness is the first step to breaking free!

- TWO-MINUTE WINS

Knock out super short, manageable tasks during waiting periods to maintain momentum and reduce that "*waiting paralysis*"—reply to an email, load the dishwasher, or lay out your clothes for tomorrow. These micro-accomplishments are **productive**.

- MORNING MEETINGS = LESS WAITING

Schedule appointments and meetings in the morning—your ADHD brain doesn't have time to spiral if the day starts with action. Plus, who has energy to overthink at 9 AM? Get it done and leave the afternoon for crushing snacks and productivity!

SENSORY OVERLOAD

When the world feels **too loud**, bright, or busy, and your brain waves a white flag, making you want to escape or shut down to protect your peace.

- NOISE-CANCELING HEADPHONES

Block out the chaos and create your personal soundscape. Silence is golden, but a curated playlist can be pure platinum.

- SUNGLASSES INDOORS

Harsh lighting got you squinting? Rock those shades inside. Who cares if it's unconventional? *Your comfort, your rules.*

- CREATE A SENSORY SAFE SPACE

Set up a cozy corner as your sensory sanctuary. Keep it simple—dim lighting, weighted blanket or soft pillows, and an essential oils diffuser with calming scents like lavender or eucalyptus. Add a white noise machine—and make it your own **recharge station**—when the world gets too loud.

SENSORY SENSITIVITY

Like having "*ADHD allergies*" to textures, sounds, or smells, where even the smallest trigger can **hijack** your focus, leaving you hyper-aware but easily overwhelmed in overstimulating environments.

- DIY SENSORY KIT

It's your survival kit for when the world feels like It's on max volume.

-Earplugs to mute the chaos
-Tinted glasses to dim the drama
-A soft scarf for cozy vibes
-A lavender roller for instant "chill"
-Bonus points for fidget toys—they're small but mighty!

- ADVOCATE FOR YOUR NEEDS

Let people know what sets you off—politely, of course. "*Hey, that perfume is lovely, but it's making my brain tap out. Mind if we crack a window?*"

- MICRO ESCAPES FOR SENSORY RELIEF

Overwhelmed? Step out for 5 minutes and let your senses **recalibrate**. Try pacing barefoot on grass, running cold water over your hands, or finding a quiet spot to pretend you're on a deserted island.

OVERSTIMULATION SHUTDOWN

When sensory or emotional overwhelm feels so *intense* that it leaves you *frozen* and withdrawn—it's your mind's emergency "pause" button, flipping you into **survival mode.**

Often unfairly mistaken for laziness, it's actually your mind's way of protecting itself from the world's overload.

- MINDFUL BREATHING

Practice deep, deliberate breaths to calm your nervous system. Inhale for four counts, hold for four, exhale for four. **Repeat** until the storm passes.
Even just one mindful breath can interrupt the spiral and bring you back to center.

- SET BOUNDARIES

Honor your energy by recognizing when something feels too much. Stepping away isn't avoidance—it's self-respect. Prioritizing your well-being allows you to show up as your best self. Boundaries aren't walls—they're bridges to a more balanced version of you.

- PLAN YOUR RECHARGE TIME

Overstimulation drains your mental battery fast. Schedule intentional recovery, like a long bath with calming scents or even a mini vacation to escape the chaos. It's not indulgent—it's how you reset and show up stronger for yourself and others.

STIMMING

Those small, *repetitive* movements like drumming fingers, bouncing a leg, or fidgeting that help you feel grounded and focused—when emotions or sensory input feel intense and difficult to manage.

- MINDFUL STIMMING

Focus on the sensation and rhythm of your stims to ground yourself and enhance their calming effects. It's your brain's natural way of finding balance—lean into it!

- FIDGET LIKE A PRO

Who says fidget toys are just for kids? There are sleek, grown-up versions out there—think stress balls, infinity cubes, and discreet spinners. Channel that restless energy like the stylish multitasker you are!

- MOVE WITH PURPOSE

Redirect restless energy by transforming it into intentional movement. Swap stimming for a grounding yoga flow, a quick gym session, or even a few energizing stretches.

SONGS ON REPEAT

Why listen to one song when you've already found ***the*** song? It's focus, comfort, and dopamine—all wrapped in a three-minute masterpiece on repeat until further notice...

- CREATE YOUR POWER PLAYLIST

Build a playlist that makes you feel like you've got it all together—because nothing says "*I'm adulting*" like blasting your favorite tunes while pretending you know what you're doing. Bonus points if it makes you dance around the house like no one's watching!

- EXPERIMENT WITH INSTRUMENTALS

Lyrics can be like that friend who talks non-stop during a movie—super distracting. Try lo-fi beats or instrumental tracks instead. It's like giving your brain the focus it craves, without the unsolicited commentary!

- MOVE WITH PURPOSE

If listening to the same song on repeat helps you focus or chill, own it. It's not "*stuck*," it's your brain's version of a *comfort blanket*.

CRISIS-INDUCED HYPERFOCUS

Rising to the occasion in **high-pressure** moments, solving problems with intense clarity and creativity—your hidden ADHD superpower during high-stakes challenges.

- SET BOUNDARIES IN CRISIS MODE

In a crisis, it's easy to get lost in the urgency. Set boundaries to protect your time and energy, especially when others rely on you. Take a breather, reset, and clear your head before moving on.

- SCHEDULE DOWNTIME

Your brain craves dopamine, especially in a crisis, pushing you to keep going non-stop. But you can't run on empty—schedule intentional breaks. Take a walk, stretch, or just pause for a few minutes. These breaks **recharge** you and you'll come back stronger and ready to own the day!

- CELEBRATE THE WIN

You just crushed it under pressure—that's the ADHD magic right there, turning chaos into focus! Give yourself a break, a treat, or just a moment to acknowledge how *badass* you are. Seriously, you've earned it!

RABBIT HOLE/ DEEP DIVE PHASE

Becoming laser-focused on a new hobby or interest, diving in headfirst with ***unstoppable*** excitement, only to drop it like a hot potato once the initial thrill wears off.

- DEEP DIVES = CREATIVE GOLDMINE

Instead of seeing it as a waste of time, embrace the deep dive. ADHDers often stumble upon wild ideas and innovative solutions while chasing random tangents. What looks like distraction could be your next big breakthrough.

- PRIORITIZE LIKE A PRO

Make a simple, in-your-face list of your top priorities and let it stare you down. When you start drifting down a rabbit hole, glance at that list and remember what actually needs to get done. Stay on track—your goals need your attention!

- CATCH THOSE IDEAS

Celebrate the joy of curiosity by jotting down any sparks in a notebook or app. Capture them, but remind yourself to balance it with other priorities. Later, you'll have a stash of ideas ready to revisit when the time's right.

IMPATIENCE! (INTERRUPTING OTHERS)

Blurting out during conversations because the thought feels *too exciting* to hold onto. Even when you're **trying hard** to listen and let the other person finish, your brain's already grasped their point and is halfway through formulating a response. Might come across as rudeness—it's just *impulsive enthusiasm*!

- PRACTICE ACTIVE LISTENING

Give your full attention—eye contact, a nod, and quietly repeat what they're saying in your head. Stop waiting for your turn to talk and start truly hearing them. It's like upgrading your connection —it just feels more real when you listen first.

- ACCOUNTABILITY PARTNER

Tell a friend or colleague about your goal to stop interrupting. They can give you a subtle nudge when you slip up, like a polite "*hold on*" gesture. It will be like having your own convo coach!

- OWN THE MOMENT

If you can't resist the urge to jump in, own it with something like, "*Oops, I just couldn't wait to share that!*" It's a lighthearted way to show you're aware of your impulsiveness, and it helps ease the tension while still keeping the conversation flowing.

IMPULSE BLURT

Saying your thoughts out loud before you've had a chance to *filter* them, often surprising others—or even yourself.

- PAUSE AND PONDER

Before speaking, take a deep breath and pause. Ask yourself, "*What's the intention behind this thought? Is it helpful, kind, or necessary?*" This can give you the space to communicate with **intention**, not impulse.

- SEEK FEEDBACK

Reach out to trusted friends or colleagues for honest feedback on how you communicate. This isn't about criticism—it's a chance to understand how your words impact others and discover areas where you can grow, helping you connect more authentically.

- REWARD YOUR PATIENCE

Celebrate small wins for controlling your impulses. Whether it's holding off on sending that reactive text or resisting the urge to blurt out something unfiltered in a conversation, treat yourself with a reward.

IMPULSIVE SHOPPING

Replacing emotions with random 2 AM Amazon purchases for that *sweet* dopamine hit—it feels amazing in the moment, but let's just say the excitement fades faster than the receipt does.

- LIMIT INSTANT GRATIFICATION

Turn off sales notifications or set digital boundaries to avoid impulsive buys. We've all fallen for the "50% OFF" trap, right? If it's not on your plan, just skip it.
Protect your focus (and wallet) by treating marketing pings like background noise—not urgent calls to action.

- BUDGET WITH BOUNDARIES

Budget for small, guilt-free splurges to satisfy the dopamine cravings responsibly. Allocate a fixed amount each month, and once you hit that limit, stop.

- CREATE A WISHLIST, NOT A CART

Feeling that impulse? Write it down instead. Create a wishlist and use a "cooling-off" rule: wait 24 hours. Most of the time, the urge will fade, and you'll realize you didn't actually want it.
Bonus: It feels way more rewarding to buy something you still want a day (or week) later.

DOOMSCROLLING

Bingeing a show, getting lost in a game, or losing track of time endlessly swiping on your phone.

It's part **escape**, part dopamine boost—a deep dive into a Rabbit Hole you didn't plan to explore.

- DELETE SOCIAL MEDIA APPS ENTIRELY

Radical? Maybe. But removing apps like Instagram, Facebook, or TikTok from your home screen forces you to actively search for them if needed. Try it for a week or month to reclaim your time and make room for **deeper** work and real-world connections.

- CURATE YOUR FEED

Follow accounts that make you feel inspired, motivated, or calm. Unfollow (or mute) things that fuel negativity or mindless scrolling. This can bring surprising clarity to your day and a sense of mental peace.

- TRANSFORM SCROLL TIME INTO PURPOSE

Rather than escaping through endless scrolling, use that time to nurture your growth—whether through learning, podcasts, or audiobooks. Instead of avoiding the life you have, embrace it and take steps to create the life you truly desire.

RESTLESSNESS/SLEEPLESSNESS

That constant itch to move, fidget, or find something stimulating, especially in *slow* or *restrictive* situations like meetings or long lines.

And when the world finally quiets down, your brain throws a 3 a.m. dance party instead of letting you sleep.

• CALMING RITUALS BEFORE BED

Stop scrolling and give your brain a break. Set aside a few minutes—just 10—and dive into something calming: light a candle, read a page, and let the chaos of the day melt away. It's not about perfection; it's about making your brain realize: "*Oh, it's time to chill now*".

• CREATE A SLEEP SANCTUARY

Make your bedroom a rest-only zone. Keep it cool, dark, and quiet. No more late-night phone scrolls or binge-watching. Blackout curtains and white noise machines are your new sleep sidekicks—watch your body go from restless to restful in no time.

• CONSISTENCY IS KEY

Set a sleep schedule and stick to it—same wake-up, same bedtime. Your body will stop playing hard to get and actually fall asleep when it's supposed to. A few weeks in, and you'll wake up feeling like a sleep master, because you are...

OUT-OF-THE-BOX THINKING (INNOVATIVE PROBLEM-SOLVING)

Tackling challenges with creative, *unconventional solutions* that others might overlook—ADHD's gift for seeing the world differently.

It's no wonder many of us excel in **entrepreneurship,** driven by a bold willingness to take risks.

- EMBRACE WILD BRAINSTORMS

Let your mind roam free—nothing's too wild. Jot down any idea, no matter how unconventional. Remember when a crazy idea surprised everyone with its result? Creativity thrives when you break boundaries.

- COLLABORATE AND REFINE

Instead of sticking to your usual team or industry, try bouncing ideas off people from different backgrounds or areas of expertise. Sometimes, a new voice or viewpoint is all it takes to see things in a completely different way. Collaborating helps turn raw concepts into solid plans.

- FOLLOW YOUR CURIOSITY

Innovative ideas often come from passions and curiosities. Use this gift to tackle challenges creatively, but pair it with focus strategies.

HYPER-CREATIVITY

Those intense bursts of imaginative brilliance where your brain lights up with **innovative** ideas, artistic projects, or unique solutions to problems—often sparked by spontaneity and the excitement of diving into something new.

- CAPTURE EVERY IDEA

Don't let that sudden burst of creativity slip away! Keep a quick-access notebook or voice recorder app to jot down thoughts, even if they seem random. Some of the *best ideas* come from those late-night flashes of inspiration.

- PRIORITIZE YOUR BEST IDEAS

When your mind's racing with a hundred concepts, pick the **top 3** to explore. Start by developing one fully before moving to the next. It's easy to get lost in the "what-if" whirlwind, but narrowing it down will make your creative sparks count.

- HARNESS YOUR IDEA FACTORY

Your ADHD brain connects dots in unique ways, making you a natural *innovator*. While that creativity is a superpower, it can also lead to scattered focus. Channel that energy by setting small, clear goals for each idea to avoid getting lost in the whirlwind.

PRODUCTIVITY BURSTS

Those short, ***high-energy*** sprints where you accomplish a ton, usually sparked by interest or urgency, and often followed by a *crash* that demands a much-needed recharge phase.

• SHORT SPRINTS, BIG WINS

Embrace intense, focused bursts for 15–30 minutes, then take a break. It's not about long hours, but making every minute count. You'll be amazed at what can get done in just a few focused moments.

• ALIGN WITH YOUR ENERGY

Some days you're a morning person, other days you're a night owl. Work with your *natural* rhythm and schedule your most demanding tasks during your peak energy times—don't try to force productivity when you're running on **empty**.

• PAIR TASKS WITH REWARDS

Make it a game—finish a burst of work, then **reward** yourself with something small and enjoyable. Whether it's a snack, a 5-minute scroll through social media, or a quick walk outside, incentives keep you energized and on track.

CLUTTER BLINDNESS

Your brain tunes out the mess completely, leaving it invisible until, out of nowhere, it becomes an <u>*overwhelming*</u> mountain you can't ignore.

• DECLUTTER WITH PURPOSE

Regularly go through your space and clear out what you no longer need. A tidy environment reduces mental clutter and makes it easier to keep track of both things and people.
Clearing space outside of you often creates space within you, too.

• DECLUTTER AS YOU GO

Picture this: you actually put away items after use and sort mail immediately. Build small decluttering **habits** into your **daily** routine, and watch your world feel lighter.Consistency—not perfection—is what keeps the chaos from piling back up

• CLEAR IT AND CHEER IT!

After you clear up a small mess, reward yourself. A little dopamine boost will help your brain stay engaged in the process. Maybe a cup of your favorite tea or a 5-minute dance break. Because yes, *you* earned it.

THE ADHD TAX

That frustrating *EXTRA* cost we pay for missed deadlines, late fees, lost items, or impulse buys—basically, the **price** of living in a brain that doesn't always play by the rules.

- AUTOMATE IT

Let tech handle it! Auto-pay your bills and set recurring reminders for everything from birthdays to reordering necessities (so you're never out of toothpaste again!).

- BUILD AWARENESS OF ADHD TRAITS

Impulsivity, forgetfulness, and chaos are just part of the deal. By being mindful of these quirks, you can catch them before the "ADHD tax" hits. When you're about to buy that **10th** notebook or miss an appointment, give yourself a mental high-five for catching it early. Laugh it off, redirect, and save yourself the hassle! It's all part of the journey. Forgive yourself—living with ADHD is hard work.

- "NOW, NOT LATER" HABIT

Write it down, voice record, or text yourself details the **moment** they pop up. Jot it down immediately and make it a habit. Your future self will thank you.

FOOD HYPERFIXATION (MEAL REPETITION)

Eating the ***same*** meals on repeat for weeks or months because it's comforting, simple, and reduces decision fatigue—sometimes, less choice means more peace.

- LEAN INTO THE ROUTINE

Meal repetition is basically your brain's way of saying, "*Let's skip the drama!*". When you're too tired to decide, your trusty meal takes the stress out of it. Why choose when you can just hit repeat?

- CREATE A GO-TO MEAL LIST

When you're eating the same thing every day, make a list of simple meals to rotate. No more staring at the fridge like it owes you money. Just pick a meal and *move on*—it's like having a personal chef who knows exactly what you like, no questions asked!

- "SWAP" METHOD FOR VARIETY

Instead of reinventing the wheel, swap out a key ingredient in your favorite meal. Swap spinach for kale, or switch rice for quinoa. Small changes keep things *interesting*, but you won't feel like you're starting from scratch.

REACTANCE

That rebellious urge to do the exact *opposite* when someone asks you to do something you were already planning, because nothing sparks the need for autonomy like feeling micromanaged—even accidentally!

- OWN YOUR DECISIONS

Reactance grows when you feel powerless. Take back control by owning even the small choices—like what to eat or when to start your day. These small acts of agency build **confidence**, making it easier to tackle bigger decisions without resistance.

- REFRAME REQUESTS AS CHOICES

When a request lands, treat it like a menu of options—not a command. This shift lets you feel in control, maintaining your autonomy while making the decision that works best for you. Use self-talk: "*I'm choosing to do this for me, not because I was told to.*"

- EMBRACE YOUR REBELLION, THEN ZOOM OUT

Let yourself have a mini tantrum, but then snap out of it and zoom out. Remember, the bigger picture is way cooler than whatever you're resisting right now!

ADHD PARALYSIS

When the **overwhelm** hits hard, and you feel like you're stuck in mental quicksand—completely frozen and unable to move forward, **no matter** how much you want to.

It's not laziness, it's like your brain's emergency brake has been slammed on. You can see the mountain of tasks ahead, but it feels impossible to take the first step.

- TAKE THE FIRST TINY STEP

The thought of completing an entire task can be overwhelming. So, break it down into something so small it feels silly—like opening the document or writing just one sentence. Often, just starting is all you need to break through the paralysis. (For example, opening your email inbox might feel huge, but just writing *"Hi"* to start a reply can get the ball rolling.)

- USE THE "FIVE-MINUTE RULE"

Commit to doing something for just 5 minutes. No pressure to finish—just show up. You'll often find that after 5 minutes, the task becomes more manageable, and **momentum** kicks in. (Think of it like pressing play on your favorite song—you do not have to commit to listening to the whole album!)

- ACCOUNTABILITY BUDDY SYSTEM

Partner with someone who supports you and understands your challenges. Sometimes, just knowing someone else is checking in makes all the difference.

LATE DIAGNOSIS

Realizing later in life that your brain wasn't broken—just different...
It's a mix of ***relief*** *at finally understanding yourself,*
and ***grief*** *for all the struggles and self-blame you endured without knowing why...*

- CELEBRATE YOUR NEW BEGINNING

Finally knowing you have ADHD is a powerful moment! Celebrate the newfound clarity—no more questioning why things have been hard.
(*Imagine the weight lifting off your shoulders when you realize it's not you, it's ADHD. Give yourself permission to feel that relief.)*

- CONNECT WITH OTHERS WHO "GET IT"

Join ADHD communities to find others who understand your journey. They've walked the same path, and their stories might resonate deeply. (*You're not alone; there are so many of us...)*

- EMBRACE SELF-COMPASSION

It's never too late to learn about your strengths and how to use them. Your journey is unique, and now that you have the **key** to understanding yourself better, it's time to embrace your growth.
(*This isn't a late start; it's the right start! Be kind to yourself as you step into this new chapter of self-awareness.)*

Reflection Page

What's one thing you now understand about yourself that you didn't before reading this book?

Reflection Page

How has your perspective shifted on what it means to live with ADHD?

If you could go back and tell your younger self one thing after reading this book, what would it be?

Paradoxes

Living with ADHD is like navigating a world of **constant contradictions**—where your mind can race with *brilliance*, but sometimes the simplest tasks feel impossible to accomplish.

These paradoxes are not just quirks of the ADHD brain. They're a reflection of the **powerful blend of strengths and challenges** that shape how you experience the world, making every day an unpredictable adventure.

- I need structure, *but I'm allergic to being told what to do.*

- I crave routine, *but too much predictability bores me out of my mind.*

- I can't focus on tiny tasks, *but give me only ONE thing to do— and I'm unstoppable.*

- I think better in a clean space, *but I can never keep it clean.*

- I start things with fireworks, *but finishing feels more like a maze.*

- I crave attention, *but a crowd drains my soul faster than my phone battery.*

- I'm loud and energetic, *yet peace and quiet are my true love.*

- I'm disorganized, *but my ideas are nothing short of genius.*

- I can't organize to save my life, *but I'll obsess over every tiny detail until it's perfect.*

- I'm impulsive, *but I overthink my next move like a chess master.*
- I seek stimulation, *but too much feels like my brain's on overload.*
- I love spontaneity, *but planning saves my sanity.*
- I crave control, *but put me in a decision-making spot and I will freeze.*
- I can laser focus on something, *but forget everything else.*
- I do everything at once, *but nothing ever gets finished.*
- I need a break, *but feel guilty every second I take one.*
- I need help, *but I'll refuse it until I'm at my breaking point.*
- One minute I'm on top of the world, *the next minute I'm running on empty.*

Real ADHD Facts, No Filter

These are the things **no one told you when you got your diagnosis**—because most people don't even know them. Some of these facts will explain things you've felt your whole life but couldn't name. Others **might hit harder**, because they show just how deeply ADHD can shape your energy, emotions, and identity.

They're not just interesting—they're the missing pieces that make the whole picture finally make sense.

You're not imagining it.
And you're ***definitely*** *not alone.*

- There are **three types of ADHD**: inattentive, hyperactive-impulsive, and combined—and **each can look completely different** in daily life.

- ADHD is not a lack of attention—it's a **dysregulation of attention**.

- It's a **neurodevelopmental condition**, not a personality flaw or behavioral issue.

- Neuroimaging research has shown both **structural** (size/volume) **and functional** (activity/connectivity) differences in key brain regions in individuals with ADHD.

- ADHD **impacts executive functions** like planning, prioritizing, and emotional regulation.

- **Dopamine plays a central role**—it's part of what drives the need for novelty.

- ADHD **brains seek stimulation**—which can look like impulsivity or risk-taking.

- **Sleep issues** are extremely common in ADHD.
- **Emotional regulation** is often harder than focus.
- People with ADHD **often forget what they know** under pressure.
- It affects **both children and adults**—it doesn't disappear with age.
- ADHD has a **strong hereditary link**—it often runs in families, with parents or siblings showing similar traits.
- For years, ADHD research focused mostly on boys, causing generations of **women to be missed or misdiagnosed.**
- Girls and women **tend to internalize symptoms**, which means their ADHD may present differently.
- **Many women aren't diagnosed until adulthood**—often after their child is diagnosed, triggering a **self-realization.**

- Women are more likely to be **misdiagnosed—often with anxiety, depression, or even borderline personality disorder**—before ADHD is ever considered.

- Women of color are even **less likely to be diagnosed, due to systemic bias, stigma, and healthcare disparities.**

- **Perfectionism and burnout are common coping mechanisms** in women with undiagnosed ADHD—they often become "overachievers" to cover up internal chaos.

- ADHD can impact **self-esteem and identity deeply in women**, especially those who've spent their lives wondering why things felt harder for them.

- **Many women with ADHD experience chronic shame**, especially around home management, parenting, or forgetfulness—despite **trying extremely hard.**

- Late-diagnosed women often **experience a profound grief over years of misunderstood struggles and missed support**—this grief is real and valid.

- Rejection sensitivity dysphoria (RSD) **can hit especially hard in women who were raised to be "pleasers" or overly self-critical.**

Now, let's wrap up on a positive note...

- *You can have ADHD and **still be high achieving**.*
- *People with ADHD tend to be **incredibly creative and intuitive.***
- *ADHD isn't just about deficits—**it comes with strengths like** hyperfocus, creativity, empathy, and big-picture thinking, **especially when properly supported.***
- *With support, strategies, and self-compassion, ADHD can be your **superpower.***
- *People with ADHD often **thrive in dynamic environments** due to their adaptability and quick thinking.*

Crushing ADHD Statistics

Some truths hit harder when seen in numbers. These statistics aren't here to scare you—they're here **to wake up awareness**. Behind every percentage is a real person navigating systems that weren't built for ADHD brains.

You are not the stat—you're the shift.
Let these numbers move you, not define you.

- **Over 50% of adults with ADHD also experience anxiety disorders. ***

- Women are **three times less** likely to be diagnosed than men.

- Around 33% of adults with ADHD never complete college.

- **One in eleven women** are estimated to have ADHD—with many remaining undiagnosed.

- Women are diagnosed with ADHD **10+ years later** than men.

- ADHD costs the U.S. economy over **$100 billion annually** in lost productivity.

- Adults with ADHD are **more likely to be unemployed** or underemployed.

- **60% of adults** with ADHD have struggled with romantic relationship stability.

➤ Source: Kessler, R. C. et al. (2006). "The prevalence and correlates of adult ADHD in the United States." American Journal of Psychiatry.

- **80% of adults** with ADHD report chronic procrastination.
- People with ADHD are **2–3x more likely** to experience depression. *
- There's a **74% chance** a child with ADHD has a biological relative with it. *
- Less than **20% of women** with ADHD receive proper diagnosis or treatment.
- **ADHD is underdiagnosed in BIPOC communities** by 40–60%. *
- People with ADHD are **more likely to have chronic health issues** due to burnout and overwhelm.
- Suicide rates are **notably higher** among undiagnosed or unsupported ADHD adults—especially women. *

➤ Source: Biederman, J. et al. (1991). "Clinical correlates of ADHD in adults."
(Also supported by NIMH and CHADD summaries.)
➤ Source: Faraone, S. V. et al. (2005). "The heritability of ADHD: A meta-analysis of twin studies." Source: Coker, T. R. et al. (2016). "Racial and ethnic disparities in ADHD diagnosis and treatment." Pediatrics.
➤ Source: Ljung, T. et al. (2014). "Attention-deficit/hyperactivity disorder and risk of suicide." Journal of the American Academy of Child & Adolescent Psychiatry.

- Adults with ADHD are up to 3 times more likely to develop substance use disorders compared to the general population. *

- Estimates suggest that up to 25% of people in prison have ADHD—most undiagnosed or untreated *

➤ Source: Wilens, T. E., & Morrison, N. R. (2011). "The intersection of ADHD and substance abuse." Current Opinion in Psychiatry
➤ Source: Young, S. et al. (2015). "A meta-analysis of the prevalence of ADHD in incarcerated populations." Psychological Medicine.

References:
Sources include data from the CDC, NIMH, CHADD, Journal of Clinical Child & Adolescent Psychology, Journal of the American Academy of Child & Adolescent Psychiatry, peer-reviewed ADHD research (including Russell Barkley, Ph.D.), and summaries provided by ADDitude Magazine and WebMD.

Trusted ADHD Resources

For deeper support, ongoing education, and community—these are the go-to voices in ADHD:

United States – Leading ADHD Resources:
CHADD (Children and Adults with ADHD)
National nonprofit | Education, advocacy, and support
www.chadd.org
ADDitude Magazine
Trusted ADHD media resource | Strategies, expert Q&As, personal stories
www.additudemag.com
ADDA (Attention Deficit Disorder Association)
Support for adults with ADHD | Webinars, peer groups, online resources
www.add.org
Understood.org
Nonprofit focused on learning & attention differences | ADHD tools for parents & adults
www.understood.org
Russell Barkley, Ph.D. – ADHD Expert Researcher
Leading authority in clinical ADHD research & education
www.russellbarkley.org

Canada – ADHD Resources:
CADDAC (Centre for ADHD Awareness, Canada)
National Canadian organization | Education, advocacy, diagnosis resources
www.caddac.ca
CADDRA (Canadian ADHD Resource Alliance)
Primarily for clinicians, but includes public resources & treatment guidelines
www.caddra.ca

● *Global ADHD Resources:*

World Federation of ADHD

International scientific body | Publishes global guidelines, promotes research

🔗 *www.adhd-institute.com*

■ *United Kingdom – ADHD Resources*

ADHD UK

U.K.-based charity | Support, awareness, resources, and community events

🔗 *www.adhduk.co.uk*

ADDISS (ADHD Information Services)

National ADHD charity | Parent & adult resources, training, and advocacy

🔗 *www.addiss.co.uk*

ADHD Europe

Network of European patient advocacy organizations | Promotes ADHD awareness across EU

🔗 *www.adhdeurope.eu*

■ *Australia – ADHD Resources*

ADHD Australia

National organization | Advocacy, education, and health system navigation

🔗 *www.adhdaustralia.org.au*

ADHD Foundation Australia

Resources for families, schools, and adults | Public awareness and support

🔗 *www.adhdfoundation.org.au*

Acknowledgments

To **Professor Sima Paribakht, PhD**—*thank you for your time, care, and thoughtful encouragement along the way.*

To those who shared their time and thoughts, and genuine intention to help me along the way—your kindness stayed with me, and I'm so thankful:

Eric Hornak
Founder/Coordinator Denver-Metro CHADD
Serving Denver and the Front Range for over 15 years

Rabbi *Robyn Fryer Bodzin*
Beth Tzedec Congregation

***Chad M. Houvouras*, M.Ed**
Instructional Coach OCVS

Peggy Sullivan
ADHD Coach

***Daniel Jones* (The Aspie World)**
TheAspieWorld.com

Cynthia Romanzo
ADHD Coach, Certified Autism Specialist

***Elan Marko*,** Founder **(Deep Work Sprints)**
Deepworksprints.com

Acknowledgments

During the writing process, I experienced deep personal shifts and some support came from places that won't be a part of my story long-term.

Lessons came not just through encouragement, but also through contrast—reminding me of what I needed and what I no longer wanted.

For that, I hold a quiet, complex kind of gratitude...

Alisa Tangtakoune (Awakened Heart, Author) and **Kelly Mah** (mom, Traveler, Author @kellyconscious)—Your frienship, loving support, and steady belief in me were felt in all the quiet moments. You showed up in the ways that matter most, and this book carries your fingerprints in the softest, most beautiful ways.

To **Lilly, Yoko and Briana**

Thank you for being the reason I keep learning, unlearning, and holding space for who we're all becoming.

To my best friends, ***Sameer and Jill Baynton****—thank you for seeing what I couldn't yet see in myself, and for recognizing what I hadn't yet named. Your insight and support didn't just lead to a diagnosis—it led me back to myself. It opened a door that changed everything...*

You've been two of the truest and most consistent cheerleaders in my life—always reminding me who I am when I lose sight of it.

You each hold a piece of my heart

love you

Aleksandra M

To every person who discovered their ADHD later in life—you inspired this book. Your strength, resilience, and curiosity fuel this entire project.

To the ADHD community online and offline—thank you for being so real, raw, and generous with your stories. You reminded me I wasn't alone and helped me find clarity when everything felt like a chaotic swirl.

To my family—thank you for your patience while I disappeared into research, writing, and rewriting (and re-rewriting). Your love kept me grounded.

To my younger self—this book is for you. For all the times you felt different and didn't know why. I see you now. And I've got your back.

Lastly, to every reader holding this book: thank you for meeting me here. I hope these pages help you feel seen, understood, and just a little more hopeful. We're not broken. We're discovering our essence.

Aleksandra M

Know someone who's still trying to **"figure it out"**? Gently share this book with them.
It might be The Thing that helps them finally put the puzzle pieces together.

Hey You:) Stay connected:
adhd.aleks@gmail.com
www.adhdrealtips.com
@adhdrealtips on Instagram

I'd love to hear your story

Acknowledgments & Resources
Many of the insights in this book are inspired by the work of ADHD experts, advocates, coaches and communities who've helped make this information more accessible.
In particular, I want to acknowledge the ongoing contributions of voices like Dr. Russell Barkley, CHADD, ADDitude Magazine, and other trusted ADHD platforms.
This book was created to simplify, personalize, and share what I've learned through research, lived experience, and the powerful stories of others. I encourage every reader to continue exploring these sources for deeper support and guidance.

Made in United States
Troutdale, OR
11/03/2026

56844891R00086